The GUBU File

Loose Talk

The GUBU File

Damian Corless

illustrated by
Michael McCarthy

WOLFHOUND PRESS

First published 1995 by
WOLFHOUND PRESS Ltd
68 Mountjoy Square
Dublin 1

© 1995 Damian Corless
Illustrations © 1995 Michael McCarthy

The material in this book has been compiled from printed and broadcast sources as listed at the end of the publication. The publishers have taken every precaution to ensure the accuracy of text, facts and citations. However the publishers disclaim responsibility for any inadvertent errors or inaccuracies but will be happy to correct or amend in future editions any that may exist.

British Library Cataloguing in Publication Data
A catalogue record for this book is available from the British Library.

ISBN 0-86327-518-4

Cover illustration: Michael McCarthy
Cover design: Slick Fish Design, Dublin
Typesetting: Wolfhound Press
Printed in the UK by Cox & Wyman Ltd, Reading, Berks.

Contents

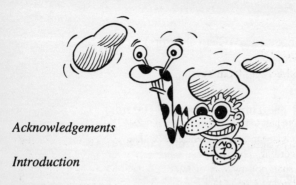

Acknowledgements

Introduction

Age Ten Is Generally Accepted In This Business
(For The Love Of Reason)   9

Perity With Steeling (Immortal Words)   15

Risks With Sex (Famous Last Words)   19

We Are Not Swedes . . . . (You Don't Say)   20

You Have To Be Mental (True Confessions)   22

Specialises In Naughty Nun (Privates On Parade)   27

What Do You Call A Female Cow? (Questions & Answers)   28

Speake Swooped Like A Piranha (Sports Illustrated)   31

We Call It Bumblefuck (As Seen From Abroad)   33

Something Wrong In The State Of Holland (Identity Crises) 36

Everybody Should Try To Get On (The High Moral Ground)   38

A Detergent Against Crime (Words Fail Them)   40

Violence Delays Peace (Headline News)   44

Heggald O' Heggald! (Native Wit)   47

Float The Goat's Head (Clerical Errors)   48

The Next U2 (Crystal Ball Gazing)   49

Bicycles All The Time (Occupational Hazards)   50

Things Always Seem To Go Wrong (Sob Stories)   51

Legs Missing (Life's A Pitch)   52

Dogs With Worms (Eye Of The Beholder)   54

Terminal Knitwear (Take Note)   56

A Thousand Camels (Mature Recollections)   57

Tons Of Freckles (Ad Hocking)   59

Bishop! Bishop! (Ulster Says . . .)   60

Livers And Lakes (Freudian Slips)   62

I Get A Caddy (Ouch!)   65

Drink And Play Bingo (It's A Man's World)   67

But You Told Me To (Strange Exchanges)   70

Sources   73

Acknowledgements

For providing invaluable feedback on the work in progress: Mary Corless, Jack Broder, Ivan Corless, Djinn Gallagher, Mary Walsh, Anne Marie Corless, Siobhan Cronin, Martin Corless, Arthur Mathews, Graham Linehan and, last but most, Adrienne Murphy.

To the hunters and collectors whose pioneering work in this field formed the bedrock for this tome: Liam Mackey, Declan Lynch, George Byrne, Liam Fay, Eamonn McCann and Conor O'Clery.

Miscellaneous thanks to: Seamus Cashman, Kevin Hamilton, Michael and Michael at K.C.D., Bart & Helen, Emmett & Pam, Ian O'Doherty, Sean D'Angelo, Justin Green, *In Dublin*, Paul Wonderful, Sean Quinn, and all at Wolfhound Press.

For Kay and Martin.

Introduction

Grotesque. Unbelievable. Bizarre. Unprecedented. The GUBU is an endearing feature of Irish public life. It flowers in the contorted logic of elected representatives, in the mean-spirited salvos of sectarianism, in the caterwauling of football crazies and in the earnest utterances of upstanding citizens.

Loose Talk: The GUBU File is a bewildering compendium of true confessions, Freudian slip-ups, lies, *bon mots*, naked affronts and chronic outbreaks of foot-in-mouth. The GUBU doesn't respect age, sex or status: its perpetrators include the great and the good, the bad and the ugly.

The contents of this book are guaranteed 100% Irish (under the grandmother rule).

Damian Corless, September 1995

AGE TEN IS GENERALLY ACCEPTED
IN THIS BUSINESS
(For The Love Of Reason)

I always get letters from people when I call Galway a town —
although I never do.

> *JOHN BOWMAN,* Day By Day, *RTE radio*

**Some of my friends are Protestants and some are Catholics, but if
there was an economical service they'd all go.**

> *Caller to* **Gerry Ryan Show,** *RTE radio*

When I said they'd scored two goals, of course I meant they'd scored
one.

> *RTE commentator GEORGE HAMILTON*

The events of the last year have established the identity of Northern
Ireland. People now know where Ulster is.

> *Northern Ireland Tourist Board spokesman finds a positive side to the
> outbreak of The Troubles, 1970*

Somebody there has put one and one together and come up with two.

> *Irate lobbyist on* Morning Ireland, *RTE radio*

Waiting lists are a very unreliable measure of the availability of
hospital services.

> *Health Minister RORY O'HANLON*

Shane MacGowan is off the drink now. He just drinks wine.

Record company spokesperson

One of my interests is ferns and a few years ago we tried to develop a fern collection. We put in forty or fifty new ferns. In the first week we lost nine plants! They just disappeared. And the next week we lost another nine. They were the choicest ones. I thought that was good, because up until then we thought nobody was interested in ferns.

Director of Dublin's Botanical Gardens, JIM SYNOTT

That mail used to be handled by hand, now it's handled manually.

Chief Executive of An Post, JOHN HINES, outlines new efficiency measures

My left foot is not one of my best.

Northern Ireland footballer SAMMY McILLROY

It's usually girls who tell me I'm sexist. You'd never have a fella telling me I'm sexist.

Comedian BRENDAN O'CARROLL

All George Best and I have in common is that we were born in the same area, discovered by the same scout and played for the same club.

NI international NORMAN WHITESIDE plays disassociation football

Busking does not exist; the busker is a chocolate bar.
Garda press spokesperson announcing clampdown on street musicians

Michael and Conary O'Cleary, Peregrine Cucory, Ferfeasa O'Mulconry. Yes. The names of the Four Masters who chronicled the events of Irish history in 1616. And I'm sure that many Donegal people wish that they could be here in Croke Park today!
Commentator MICHAEL O'MUIRCHEARTAIGH sets a poser for the Donegal selectors on All Ireland Final day

Clearly we're not dealing with normal supply and demand. What we are dealing with in Dublin is an audience that feels we are obliged to subsidise our concerts when we play here. And clearly they're right.
U2 manager PAUL McGUINNESS resigns himself to an expensive sort of homecoming

Most of the things I've done are my own fault, so I can't feel guilty about them.
Football's original wild child, GEORGE BEST, wrestles with his conscience and wins

Tax evasion might be a sin but tax avoidance is not. And how do you know the difference? D'ya see, if you don't know the difference, how could it be a mortal sin?
OLIVER J. FLANAGAN TD taxes the intellect

The government is not strong enough to either win or lose.
Political analyst ROBERT FISK to RTE's Pat Kenny

I'll give it 10 out of 20 . . . Go out and buy it!
>*Record reviewer MIKE RYAN caught in two minds on* The Beatbox

The referendum went as most people hoped it would.
>Irish Times *editorial displays an acute understanding*
>*of the democratic process*

Ladies and gentlemen, we apologise for the delay — it is due to the fact that we are ten minutes early.
>*Platform announcement, Thurles railway station*

If people evaluate the programmes, in logic they will come to us — if logic means anything in politics, which I tend to doubt.
>*Soon-to-be-former Taoiseach, GARRET FITZGERALD,*
>*lays the groundwork for a moral victory*

The last move takes place immediately, the others in the coming weeks.
>Irish Times *reports changes in Dept of Foreign Affairs*

Well, you wouldn't favour age two. And you wouldn't favour age fifteen or sixteen. So it would have to be somewhere in between, and we've plotted it on the graph at age ten.
>*JOHN CLERKIN of the Children's Protection Society accuses Fine Gael*
>*of promoting 'child sex' involving ten year olds, by dint of favouring*
>*condom sales with no age limits*

Interviewer: But why age ten? Why not nine or eleven?
Clerkin: Well, age ten is generally accepted in this business.

The reason I went to South Africa is that when I was a young lad I used to collect silver paper and send it off to the black babies, and I always wondered what they did with it. So I went to South Africa to find out, and discovered that they make money with it. So I took it back.
>*Irish showbiz star on entertaining the apartheid regime*

It's not really that large a house. There are four bedrooms, a kitchen and two bathrooms on the top two floors, two main reception rooms and a music room on the first floor, and a study, formal dining room and kitchen on the ground floor — it's the basement rooms which give it the extra space of a big house.

Modest homeowner to Irish Times

This referee frightens me because he's likely to give something of great consequence. Hopefully to us.

RTE soccer pundit RAY TREACY

I like a lot of Elvis Presley's old songs in that they're very, very sentimental — the lyrics in them are the same as Chris De Burgh.
Cyclist STEPHEN ROCHE

The kind air hostess offered me a glass of brandy, which I declined. Apparently, I could get plastered drunk and become a nuisance and a danger, or I could pop pills or shoot heroin, but I could not smoke.

Fr MICHAEL CLEARY flies off the handle following a one hour
'no smoking' flight to Britain

There was never sex in Ireland before television.

OLIVER J. FLANAGAN, TD

Clap your feet!

BERNIE of The Nolan Sisters

British Army bomb disposal squads who attempt to defuse car bombs early and before areas are properly evacuated will be responsible for endangering civilian lives.

IRA statement, 1988

Nothing to write home about — unless you have a postcard.

RTE commentator PHILIP GREENE on Shelbourne vs Athlone Town

The elderly could be deprived of their Vitamin C.

Fine Gael TD ALICE GLENN opposes sanctions against apartheid South Africa at a meeting of the Joint Committee on Development Co-Operation, 1986

Ian [Snodin] and I have both been out injured. He's put on weight and I've lost it, and vice versa.

Footballer RONNIE WHELAN

I'm very popular in Israel because of my big nose.

Singer JOE DOLAN

PERITY WITH STEELING
(Immortal Words)

He jumped in the air and knocked his wig off. He put it on again as if nothing had happened. A true professional.

JOE MAC of the Dixies showband in praise of Dickie Rock

The best way to see Donegal is to get as high as you can.

Singer VAL DOONICAN recommends a healthy altitude

Someone has been spreading allegations, and I know who the allegators are.

Drogheda Urban District Councillor

Healthy people are advised to stay in bed, drink plenty of fluids and call the doctor if the symptoms are severe.

Irish Times *during 'flu epidemic*

He's pulling him off. The Spanish manager is pulling his captain off!

RTE's GEORGE HAMILTON as Butreguanio comes off against Ireland

Eric Clapton's new album, *Journeyman*, is one of those let's-everyone-give-a-hand jobs.

Rock critic RODERICK O'CONNOR, Evening Press

And so we leave this beautiful place with the glorious smell of pig in our nostrils.

DONNCHA O'DULAING signs off Donncha's Sunday, *RTE radio*

The three great success stories of Irish society: the Blarney Woollen Mills, the Kerry Co-Op and U2.

Broadcaster LIAM O'MURCHU

People keep going on about tit for tat murders, but as far as I'm concerned it's been all tat and not enough tit.

Loyalist paramilitary on BBC NI

The Romanian people were very generous but they know very little about Ireland. 'They never heard of Dev or Willie Cosgrave, but they know all about Joe Dolan.'

Meath Councillor FERGUS MULDOON in The Irish Times

I want to tell you about the Co-Operative movement. You'll get fuck all co-operation.

Tony O'Reilly is greeted on his first day as Head of the Milk Marketing Board by Co-Op leader

The idea is all well and good in theory, but tell me this, who is going to feed them?

Wicklow Councillor objects to a proposal to boost tourism by putting gondolas on the Blessington lakes

The Irish Finance Minister, Ruairy Quinn argued the case for the Irish punk to be revalued upwards beyond perity with steeling . . . We are prepared to let the Irish pound rise above party, he said.

The Indonesia Times *takes an unorthodox line on the punt/sterling parity issue*

Weather bulletin for Friday, 19th August 1991. General situation: A cold front is moving erotically southeastwards over Ireland.

Met. office report sends temperatures soaring

We are not prepared to stand idly by and be murdered in our beds.

Rev IAN PAISLEY refuses to take the Fenian threat lying down

Mass demonstrations in Berlin and Prague were echoed again in Naas on Thursday night as 200 townspeople protested outside the Town Hall against higher rates.

The Leinster Leader *puts the meltdown of the Soviet Bloc into perspective*

Life is a speckled cat.

Media guru EOGHAN HARRIS expresses dotty felines

Jaysus, there's confidence for you.

Labour TD FRANK CLUSKY reacts to the appointment of Paddy Lawlor as Fianna Fáil Director of Elections

Maybe it's a good idea. I was worrying unnecessarily about the problems of the country.

Fianna Fáil's Dr JOHN O'CONNELL packs up his troubles as his Dáil seat slips away in the 1987 elections

If I drop him I'll apologise.

Fianna Fáil TD BEN BRISCOE reassures the mother of a baby he's brandishing

RISKS WITH SEX
(Famous Last Words)

We're in an era of time when self-control seems to have been put aside as a value.

Bishop EAMON CASEY prior to becoming better known as
'Father' Eamon Casey

I'm as sexual as anyone else and there are a thousand ways in which I express that sexuality.

Bishop EAMON CASEY

I am Superman.

MARTIN CAHILL, the late General, tempts fate

The Provos are very efficient: they must be rated as one of the best terrorist organisations in the world.

UDA Chief JOHN McMICHAEL, 1986, later killed by the IRA

I'm always surprised at the amount of people who take risks with sex.

Irish Harley St doctor TOM COURTNEY recommends safe sex
practices to the readers of In Dublin *magazine. This stance was*
somewhat undermined shortly afterwards when he was jailed
for drugging a succession of female patients
and having sex with them

There is a concerted effort to convince millions of people . . . that they will be outcasts of Irish society if they do not become soccer fanatics next June. It is largely a commercial marketing ploy.

Evening Herald GAA writer EUGENE McGEE cautions against
embracing the soccer fad in the run-up to Italia '90

WE ARE NOT SWEDES . . . .
(You Don't Say)

Whatever else we are in this country, we are not Swedes and we are not Danes.

GARRET FITZGERALD taps the pulse of the Irish electorate

If you're a fifty pence piece in a pile of ten pence pieces you have to shine so much brighter in order to be noticed.

U2's BONO coins a singular phrase

They're not like the Shelbourne lads.

Former Irish manager EOIN HAND summarises his difficulties settling in as coach of South African side Amazulu FC

Obviously, there's been a lot of atrocities off the pitch.

The Republic's ALAN McLOUGHLIN tackles the Northern conflict

His strength, or strengths, are his strength.

Boxing pundit MICK DOWLING on Irish Olympic hopeful Paul Douglas

People are allowed to bring 200 cigarettes through customs from Duty Free, but not cannabis.

Justice WINDLE explains a fine point of law to U2's Adam Clayton

A husband who assaults his wife on their honeymoon and then threatens to strangle her does not seem to be a husband any lady would want.

Justice FRANK ROE adjourning a domestic case

I don't think the pornographic video is suitable for teenagers.

Writer JOHN B. KEANE

It's time he gave you one, Mrs Dukes.

Switzers' short-lived ad for in-store credit cards

I appeal to them [the Jews and Muslims] to settle their differences in accordance with Christian principles.

Taoiseach LIAM COSGRAVE

The party has an annual Ard Fheis every year.

SEAN TREACY of Fianna Fáil

This is the only country in the world where it's taken nineteen years to get a one-man bus service for Dublin city.

JOE REA of the Irish Farmers' Organisation

Expertise in the bedroom must be matched by similar expertise in the kitchen.

Dr A. R. DENNIS to meeting of the Christian Family Movement

YOU HAVE TO BE MENTAL
(True Confessions)

You have to be mental to join Youth Defence.

Youth Defence activist, JODY McDONAGH

All I need is a bed, a toilet, a chair and a drinks cabinet.

Singer SHANE MacGOWAN

Where would I like to be buried? I'd like to be buried up to my balls in Bibi Baskin.

Caller to Gerry Ryan Show

What we are doing is in the interest of everybody, bar possibly the consumer.

Aer Lingus spokesman enters a spot of turbulence

All that pseudo-intellectual stuff about ideals, and why you do it, that's all clap-trap.

Fianna Fáil's PADRAIG FLYNN reflects on his calling as a TD

Normally in a movie I'm in love with the truth, Richard Burton or a camel.

PETER 'Lawrence Of Arabia' O'TOOLE

You learn a lot about women from dressing up in women's clothes.

U2's ADAM CLAYTON

When I was very young I wanted to be a belly dancer.

OLIVIA O'LEARY quoted in Magill TV Guide *(in fact she wanted to be a ballet dancer)*

The fact that we sell a lot of records doesn't mean that we are any good.

BONO of U2

I come alive after midnight chimes. Like Dracula. That's when you see the real Hurricane . . . The trouble is my wife doesn't understand me. . . .

Hellraising snooker star ALEX HIGGINS

It's very nice, you feel like you've been able to leave something behind.

> *Broadcaster GLORIA HUNNIFORD, of a visit to the toilets of*
> *Buckingham Palace*

Normally you do it on the descent and it depends on the wind . . . If we gotta piss we gotta piss and it doesn't matter who's there beside you.

> *Cyclist STEPHEN ROCHE*

If you did bribe a TD there is absolutely nothing he could do for you. TDs have so little influence.

> *Fine Gael TD MAURICE MANNING*

The surest way to ensure that nothing gets done is to do everything correctly, by the file . . . Everything will be clean and transparent and open and nothing will be done.

> *BRIAN LENIHAN TD's critique of Irish political culture*

A lot of us have a very strong loyalty to the half-crown.

> *Unionist MEP JOHN TAYLOR promises sterling opposition to a*
> *32-county Ireland*

The [Cork] politicians were jealous . . . They thought the Yanks were making a fool out of me but they weren't. They gave me teeth. I got a doctorate degree . . . I met a lot of punk rockers in America. They wanted me to go up and stay with them but I'd say I'd end up smoking grass and all if I did.

> *Cork Councillor BERNIE MURPHY following an official visit to the*
> *United States*

I never did drugs. That's the only thing I missed out on. I never even smoked, what to do call that oul' thing? Shit.

Fianna Fáil TD CHARLIE McCREEVY

When I went to Vegas it was the time when nobody smoked cigarettes because they were cancerous and dreadful but everybody smoked pot, dope, grass . . . Morning, noon and night we did. In fact I think that's what wrecked my throat.

TWINK recalls the big smoke of Nevada

I was never particularly high.

Super-grocer FERGAL QUINN on his lack of inches

I'd like to be as tall as Brendan O'Reilly.

GAY BYRNE wishes he was upwardly mobile

I am British through and through. When I hear Paddy jokes I laugh at them.

Rev WILLIAM McCREA

I could instance a load of fuckers whose throats I'd cut and push over a cliff, but there's no percentage in that.

CHARLES HAUGHEY TD

Only that I promised Garret [Fitzgerald] to just listen, I'd have got dug out of that bastard.

ALAN DUKES TD has unparliamentary urges about a bishop

I was considered very dangerous amongst the players.

JOHN GILES confirms Eamon Dunphy's assertion that he was a 'swift assassin' on the field

I'm not big into heavy rock.

Fianna Fáil TD PADRAIG FLYNN

Deep down I'm a very shallow person.

CHARLES HAUGHEY TD

I am not a celebrity fucker.

Gossip columnist TERRY KEANE

I've got a wonderful life. I just don't particularly enjoy it.

Comedian SEAN HUGHES

There's no chance of getting a job. All you can do is appear on television programmes and get a couple of hundred here and there.

PADDY ARMSTRONG of The Guildford Four on life after life

At this stage, if I announced that my shopping lists were available, I'd have offers immediately to adapt my shopping list into a multi-million budget film.

Novelist RODDY DOYLE

A woman to me can be attractive just by saying yes.

Cabaret singer TONY ST JAMES

I'm like a page out of the Census returns: broken down by age, sex and religion.

Broadcaster SEAN MACREAMOINN

When I left school I was the only one in my class to become a grocer . . . It came natural to me that I didn't think of security. I thought of risk-taking as part of everyday life.

FERGAL 'super' QUINN

I just do what I do and get the hell out of the place.

Broadcaster MIKE MURPHY on RTE

Finbar Nolan and them, the most I ever heard of them curing was bronchitis or a skin allergy or something like that. Faith healers have actually been with me here and they reckon that I am the best faith healer, King of the faith healers.

Dublin faith healer FRED BRADLY who claims to cure AIDS

I'd welcome death with me open arms. There's no fear because I know what's on the other side. I'll tell you what it's like. Did you ever go over the hill in a car real quick, and your stomach goes up? It's a thousand times worse than that.

Ditto

My circumference was built with a knife and fork.

RTE's man of substance DEREK DAVIS

My voice comes out pretty dead on tape, but singing is better than shovelling gravel.

JIM TOBIN of The Firehouse showband digs the music scene

I lost three people who were very close to me, all in the space of three months — Pope John, John F. Kennedy and Jim Reeves.

*Senator DONIE CASSIDY recalls a tragic youth to Arthur Mathews
of Hot Press*

The Wolfe Tones played in public for the first time ever for me, for a bottle of whiskey. Between them.

ALBERT REYNOLDS TD

In 1954 when Ireland were playing Luxembourg, they had an inside left called Fuckinger. To my eternal glee he was the best player on the pitch. He was everywhere.

Radio Eireann sports commentator PHILIP GREENE

I quit showbiz because of my utter contempt for my own musical performance.

JIM CONLAN of The Royal Showband

They fucked me.

*EAMON DUNPHY on U2 following the appearance of his much-criticised
official biography of the band*

I'm afraid wives find me rather interesting.

Snooker player ALEX HIGGINS on the hazards of jealous husbands

I can hold a note and I know I'm not ugly so, in ways, that's enough.

KEITH DUFFY of Boyzone

I told my guys nothing of what I was up to. I wrapped the deal up and then told them 'Hey, we're sponsoring the Irish soccer team!' and they went 'Oh shit!'

ARNOLD O'BYRNE, MD of General Motors (Ireland)

SPECIALISES IN NAUGHTY NUN
(Privates On Parade)

Haughey, Blaney and Boland sacked today. Horray!
Diary entry of 12 year old EMILY O'REILLY, 1970
(in fact Boland resigned)

In fairness to RTE, the only thing they ever axed was a sketch about Brian Lenihan's liver.
Comic DERMOT MORGAN recalls RTE's Scrap Saturday

ULSTER STILL SAYS NO.
Icing on the cake for birthday celebrations of Iris Robinson, wife of Democratic Unionist MP Peter Robinson

There are some well endowed men in Ireland by the looks of things.
Newscaster ANNE DOYLE reflecting on the graphic contents of her fan mail

The City Manager and his assistants regard me as a prick in the fat arse of municipal pretension.
Irish Times correspondent and environment campaigner FRANK McDONALD

Uno duce, uno voce! In other words we are having no more nibbling at my leader's bum.
Haughey Press Secretary P. J. MARA delivers the bottom line

The tits would definitely be hung up.
Irish-born drag artiste DANNY LA RUE contemplates marriage and retirement

We have a girl called Sinead O'Connor who works with us. Specialises in naughty nun.
KEN FARRELL of Dublin's Hotlips kissogram agency, six years before Sinead's naughty Pope-shredding stunt

WHAT DO YOU CALL A
FEMALE COW?
(Questions & Answers)

Larry Gogan: With what town in Britain is Shakespeare associated?
Contestant: Hamlet.

Sunshine Radio deejay: What does a newsmonger sell?
Contestant: Fish.

Larry Gogan: Name the BBC's Grand Prix commentator? . . . I'll give you a clue, it's something you suck.
Contestant: Oh, Dickie Davies!
(*Correct answer*: Murray Walker)

Larry Gogan: Where is the Taj Mahal?
Contestant: At the bottom of Nassau Street.

Interviewer: What advice would you give to runners?
Noel Carroll: Don't eat like a pig.

Larry Gogan: What was Jeeves's occupation?
Contestant: He was a carpenter.

Parisian waiter: What sort of omelette would sir like?
FAI official: An egg omelette.

Mike Murphy: Which of the Evangelists was a tax collector?
Contestant: Billy Graham.

Larry Gogan: What is the international distress signal?
Contestant: Help!

Ruth Buchannon: What is Chris Lloyd's maiden name?
Contestant: Chris De Burgh!

Larry Gogan: What do you call the eggs of a louse?
Contestant: Yolks!

Job application form: Do you support the overthrow of the government by force, subversion or violence?
Applicant: Violence.

Irish Times *reports on one individual who didn't make it to the interview stage for US government job*

Joe Duffy: **Was there much TB in the Twenties and Thirties?**
100 year old woman: **No, but we had the radio.**

Japanese TV presenter: The people of Cavan are very generous?
Niall Tobin: They may have that reputation in Japan.

Shay Healy: What do you think about when you're out there playing?
Alex Higgins: Balls. Just balls.

Ian Dempsey: What would you give Andrew and Sarah as a wedding gift?
Caller: I'd like to give Fergie AIDS and put a bomb up Andy's hole.

Pat Ingoldsby: How do homing pigeons find their way home?
Man on street: How do you find your way home when you're locked? It's the same thing, a sixth sense.

Michael Lyster: How's the leg, Kevin?
Kevin Moran: It's very fuc . . . It's very sore, Michael.

Journalist: Has your sex life improved since you became a star?
Singer Aidan Walsh: Oh no, it's got much better.

Interviewer: You've devoted a whole chapter of your book to Jimmy Greaves.
Pat Jennings: That's right. Well, what can you say about Jimmy Greaves?

Larry Gogan: What do you call a female cow? . . .

SPEAKE SWOOPED LIKE A PIRANHA
(Sports Illustrated)

I have got Gary Lineker's shirt up in my hotel room, and it's only stopped moving now.

> *Irish defender MICK McCARTHY after victory over England,*
> *European Championships, 1988*

Derry's Speake swooped like a piranha.
> ***Radio Foyle football commentator RICHIE KELLY***

If Plan A fails, try Plan A.
> *MARK LAWRENSON summarises the tactics which gained Jack's heroes*
> *an historic draw vs mighty Liechtenstein*

I missed [Nicky Perez] with some tremendous punches. The wind from them could have caused him pneumonia.

> *Boxer BARRY McGUIGAN*

You can overcome a bad marriage, you can grapple with and overcome alcoholism, but you'll never get over losing an All Ireland Final. I cried for weeks afterwards. Bill Jackson was the referee, from Roscommon, and I often wake up in the middle of the night, still, shouting 'Fuck you, Jackson!'

> *Poet and former GAA star BRENDAN KENNELLY*
> *relives a decision which went against him*

Brady's been playing inside Platini's shorts all night.

> *RTE commentator JIMMY MAGEE describes a briefs encounter*

He was one of several Spanish heroes on the day.

> *Commentator GEORGE HAMILTON as the camera follows a dejected*
> *Niall Quinn off the pitch*

I don't know who you are, but I'll call you Paddy.

> *Newly installed Republic soccer manager, JOHNNY CAREY, to*
> *home-based player Eric Barber*

They have a rating for me. We went to see *Hunt For Red October* before the last match. I got a few 9s for that — but they were the intellectuals.

> *Republic trainer and movie-picker MICK BYRNE*
> *on the team's viewing habits*

He reminds me of Rosie Henderson, who played with Drumcondra in the Fifties.

> *The mercurial skills of Brazil's Eder are put into context by pundit LIAM*
> *TUOHY during the 1982 World Cup Finals*

[The Kerry] left full back, Mick Spillane, was struck on the back of the neck by a beer bottle thrown from the terrace at the city end of the ground. Other bottles were thrown then and later, but no other player was hit. Spillane was obviously badly hurt by the blow and his game was affected . . . The Kerry officials made no issue of the incident, however, and were pleased that the match was played in a sporting spirit.

> Irish Times

WE CALL IT BUMBLEFUCK
(As Seen From Abroad)

His country's roads have centre-divided strips planted with food crops.

Los Angeles Times in an article about Irish Olympic
cyclist Gary Thompson

Bookings can be made to Ireland or Ulster.

Manchester rail guide

We've got a name for places like this. We call it Bumblefuck.

Thurles town described by an employee of English pop
group The Wonderstuff

Charlie Haughey? Didn't he used to run guns for the IRA?

MICK HUCKNALL, singer with Simply Red,
unaware of Haughey's acquittal

Our services are sometimes on the level of, not the Stone Age, but maybe the Brass Age.

Irish-based **Tass** *correspondent IGOR PONOMAREV*
compares shopping in Moscow and Dublin

Jack Charlton's team of international misfits.
> *ITV commentator in build up to Italia '90*

Stephen Roche, the only British or Irish cyclist to win the Tour De France.
> *ITV commentator cheers a bicycle made for two*

Bono, 26, is the charismatic pony-tailed singer and his rock band, U2, became Britain's most exciting act since The Beatles.
> The Sunday Times *quick to acknowledge one of their own*

Mountjoy was absolute hell, a total nightmare. The warders loathed, hated and despised me. It was the worst time of my entire life. I thought I was going to be killed, but the prisoners were all right.
> *JOHNNY ROTTEN of The Sex Pistols recalls serving one week of a six month conviction following a brawl, late-Seventies*

Men used to be children.
> *Russian translation of the line 'Ahah the men's the boys!' from the Abbey's Leningrad production of* The Great Hunger

As a kid, being Irish was being different, so I always told everybody that I was Irish. My parents had all these rebel songs on albums . . . So I just feel that I have a bit of Irish in me. I've got an Irish boyfriend, so I've had quite a bit of Irish in me quite a few times.
> *Pop star BOY GEORGE O'Dowd*

Johnny Logan, you are historical!
> *Hysterical Swiss presenter of* Eurovision

Malta gave [the Eurovision] to Ireland with the very last vote. Bastards!
> The Guardian, *1993*

I'm always suspicious of games where you're the only ones that play it.
> *JACK CHARLTON on hurling*

It looks like the sort of game that should be illegal.
> *BRETT ANDERSON of pop group Suede on hurling*

Ludicrous. Ridiculous.
> *1989 edition of* Collins Concise Dictionary *defines the word 'Irish'*

It's just real cool to be here and to meet real Irish people straight from Ireland. My family come from the Mulligan, Sheridan, O'Connell, you know what I'm saying?

EVERLAST, vocalist with American rappers House Of Pain

Moderate Catholic leader Bishop John Hume has sparked a political row in Northern Ireland by meeting the leader of Sinn Fein.

The West Australian

PRESIDENT LENIHAN BROUGHT DOWN BY SCANDAL

Facts on File: Encylopaedia Of The 20th Century

All they got in LA is sun-tanned faggots. Not like the real men you got here in Dublin.

Rock star JON BON JOVI

About two thirds of the population of Northern Ireland are immigrants from England and Scotland who believe in Protestantism. Their political organisation, the Fine Gael (United Ireland Party) stands for unification with Britain.

Beijing Review

You Irish must be nuts. Imagine Catholics killing Protestants and Protestants killing Catholics. Why don't the Catholics and Protestants get together and kill the niggers?

New York cabbie to Seamus Martin of The Irish Times

Faith and Begorra, there's no better way to begin an Irish fling than with O'Delta Airlines.

Delta Airlines brochure

Remember, all you untrained Irish lads, the tin foil is not to be used in an emergency. It is only there to stop the product from perishing.

British Labour MP JOE ASHTON commenting on the 1985 liberalisation of Ireland's condom laws. He suggested a new brand called Thick Micks

I'll be talking to the leaders of your government, the President, the Taoiseach and, of course, your Prime Minister.

US House Speaker TIP O'NEILL on Morning Ireland

SOMETHING WRONG IN THE STATE OF HOLLAND

(Identity Crises)

Congress in its good judgement has felt that this International Fund (For Ireland) will help to encourage dialogue and co-operation between Unionists and Loyalists.

> *US Ambassador designate WILLIAM FITZGERALD suggests a novel approach to achieving peace in the North*

The highlight of the night was a memorable jam session between Alec Finn and Harry Dean Stanton who plays with Paris Texas.

> *LIZ RYAN of the* Evening Herald

Singer Jerry Lee Lewis will be less than funny for a time. The veteran comedian who is the only living American awarded a Legion d'Honneur for services to the arts, broke his leg water-skiing.

> Evening Herald *delivers two celebs for the price of one*

I'm glad for the fans back in Ireland.

> *ALAN McLOUGHLIN speaking in Belfast after his famous Windsor Park equaliser sends the Republic to the 1994 World Cup Finals*

Hello Dublin!

> *DAVID BOWIE on stage in Co. Meath*

Hello London!

> *Singer STEVIE NICKS on stage in Dublin*

Sam will never die.

> *RTE presenter on the enduring appeal of* Finnegan's Wake, *not one of Sam Beckett's finest works*

Tell me Phil, why did you leave Genesis?

> *New York socialite to Derry composer Phil Coulter*

As they say in football, it's a funny old world.

> *Broadcaster RONAN COLLINS*

'The Terminator' was a man with an Irish accent [who would] terminate a man from half a mile away for money.

Consultant obstetrician LOUIS COURTNEY displays a sketchy knowledge of Arnie Schwarzenegger's most celebrated role, during an abortion debate on Questions & Answers

Like they said long ago in a story, something is wrong in the state of Holland.

Senator PASCHAL MOONEY quotes Hamlet *something rotten to the Seanad*

We do an Irish song. It's called 'Olé Olé Olé'.

Australian group Bjorn Again

. . . Stavros Niarchos, Gregory Peck, Yves Saint Laurent, Marc Bolan and Ballenciago.

Sunday Independent diarist spots a surprise guest at the wedding of Princess Caroline of Monaco in July 1978. Rocker Marc Bolan had been laid to rest the previous August

Cor, I 'ope our one ain't as long as that.

JOE KINNEAR hears Amhrán Na bhFiann *on his footballing début for the Republic*

The bird of peace — the pigeon.

Commentator JIMMY MAGEE fowls up

EVERYBODY SHOULD TRY
TO GET ON
(The High Moral Ground)

Who does that fucking nigger think he is?

*Protest organiser Kadar Asmal of the ANC comes under fire from one of
his own anti-apartheid demonstrators outside Lansdowne Road,
Ireland vs Springbox, 1970*

Chris Cary treats the Irish like I'd treat the blacks.

*'Captain' EAMONN COOKE of Radio Dublin berates the owner
of a rival pirate station*

Let us hope and trust that there are sufficient proud and ignorant people
left in this country to stand up to the intellectuals who are out to destroy
faith and fatherland.

OLIVER J. FLANAGAN TD

Fuck.

1994 Grammy winner BONO at Grammy Awards

Isn't that sort of language part of what we are?

1994 Grammy winner PADDY MOLONEY puts the case for the defence

If we even had the money to use hired muscle . . . It must cost a fortune.

NIAMH NIC MHATHUNA of Youth Defence thinking aloud

I don't criticise anybody. I just think politicians should be some kind
of . . . everybody should try to get on.

Political analysis by STEPHEN ROCHE

The fact is that there is a section of the community who are better
equipped to do this skilled work — and that happens to be the
Protestant community.

*Democratic Unionist MP PETER ROBINSON upon the opening of the
Shorts factory in Belfast, 1984*

Too close contact with the Ulster Unionist mentality affects the most healthy minds.

Irish Times *editorial, 1970*

A redundant second-rate politician from a country peopled by peasants, priests and pixies.

Broadcaster ROBERT KILROY-SILK on EU Agriculture Commissioner Ray MacSharry, in The Daily Express

I wonder if the housewife has the time for discussions. What is often called 'wallpaper radio', with time signals, may be a good answer to her problem.

DONNCHA O' DULAING, Head of Radio Features, RTE, 1970

Donncha O'Dulaing has his place. It's a small jail in Guatemala.

Comic DERMOT MORGAN

A DETERGENT AGAINST CRIME
(Words Fail Them)

As you may have seen recently, I raised the disturbing level of atmospheric pollution in the Ranelagh/Rathmines area.

Senator ALEXIS FITZGERALD comes clean in a circular to residents

Every company needs a strong, strong hand at the till . . . tiller!

Prof EDWARD CAHILL of UCC on Morning Ireland

The Minister has said they're going to bring in the Seven Horsemen of the Apocalypse.

***JIM QUIGLEY of Muintir Na Tíre on* Morning Ireland**

I will be raising the matter in the Dáil at the *ealriest* opportunity and call on the Minister to *immeidately* reverse this most heartless and callous decision.

Statement from Progressive Democrat TD MAIRIN QUILL demanding government action on ILLITERACY (my italics)

May Jesus Christ, the Son of God, in his mercy help you in good times and in bed.

Dublin wedding missalette

This is the moment I have always longed for — to walk the roads once trodden by my ancestors and to see the hillsides where they also probably roamed.

US Ambassador MARGARET HECKLER

We considered in detail, but ultimately rejected, the option of introducing, as an offence less serious than rape, the offence of engaging in sexual intercourse.

Law Reform Commission consultation paper

Next week is another day.

Progressive Democrat TD PEADAR CLOHESSY

Moules Marinere: Fresh mussels served with shite wine and cream.

Advert in Dublin Tribune

I'm having a little bit of trouble with my pronuncinations this evening.

Radio Dublin deejay

Outside HIV in Grafton Street.

GAY BYRNE plugs an appearance by Hot House Flowers
outside the HMV store

When are you going to take a photograph of my cock?

> *Louth Fianna Fáiler FRANK GODFREY, a keen fowler, attracts the attention of a photographer (and everyone else within earshot) at the opening of a school by Education Minister, Gemma Hussey*

This young man has been charged with cycling in a built-up area without a bicycle.

> *Dublin Circuit Court Judge*

The Pope is trying to eliminate people's consciences.

> *2FM news*

We need a detergent against crime.

> ***County Councillor to Marian Finucane***

All students should be sterilised before starting a microbiology experiment.

> *Demanding Leaving Cert biology paper*

Stephen's riding has been very offensive.

> *Stephen Roche's team-mate CLAUDIO CHIAPUCCI admires his attacking style*

Let this be a silent protest that will be heard throughout the country.
Limerick Mayor, TIM LEDDIN, leaves his audience speechless

There is a high level of dissatisfaction among Irish Catholics with the sermons they hear at Sunday mass ... The least favoured topics for adults and students are appeals for money, sex, politics, and drugs.

Irish Times

VIOLENCE DELAYS PEACE

(Headline News)

CASH WORRIES AN UNDER-AGE BASKETBALL

Evening Press

THOSE DISGRACEFUL MADONNA PICTURES —
FOUR PAGE SPECIAL INSIDE

Irish Sun

VIOLENCE DELAYS PEACE — LENIHAN

Irish Times

CONCERNED RAPIST WORE A CONDOM

Evening Herald

MRS REAGAN BETTER AFTER FALL

Irish Times

FANTASTIC ORGY IN SECOND HALF

*Le Journal Du Dimanche on a thrilling Ireland vs France
rugby international*

SHARING THE BURDEN OF SCHIZOPHRENIA

Irish Times

ENDANGERED WILD ANIMALS RUN AMOK IN STEPHEN'S GREEN

Dublin Evening News *fires a salvo in the circulation war*

NO NEWS TODAY

Dublin Evening News *admits defeat*

DOG SHOOTS MAN

Evening Press

TEENAGE MUTANT BINGE AT THURLES

In Dublin *at Féile '91*

WOMEN MORE POLITICAL SAYS LOO WALL STUDY

Evening Press

SA HANGS BLACKS AND WHITES TOGETHER

— A Supreme Court official said, 'There is no apartheid there'

Evening Press

'AAGH, GOD, HO': COCKROACHES SPURN THE GOKIBURI HOY-WOY

Irish Times *headline-writer in brainstorm shock!*

'YOU SHOULD BE PROSECUTED', INANE MAN IS TOLD

Roscrea Journal *(Inane is a townland in Tipperary)*

PUNIC WARS END

Irish Times

MONSIGNOR CASEY DEFENDED HUMAN RIGHTS AND AT THE
SAME TIME TREATED HIS SON WORSE THAN A DOG

La Republica *(Peru)*

RAPE MAN: I THOUGHT SHE WAS MY WIFE

Star

ILLITERARY COURSES CAN OPEN UP A WHOLE NEW WORLD

Southside Express

THE FRENCH LEFT'S TENANT

Irish Times *reports Taoiseach Fitzgerald going to stay with
Socialist President Mitterand*

CHAIRS TO BE ABOLISHED

Irish Medical Times

I.N.T.O. MEMBERS WILL ENROL FOUR YEAR OLDS

Irish Times

ALBUM IS THE THING

Evening Press

MAN KEPT ARMS UNDER BED AFTER RELATIVE'S DEATH

Irish Times

DEAD MAN INJURED IN CRASH

Irish Times

HEGGALD O' HEGGALD!
(Native Wit)

After the break we'll have more comedy in *Cheers*.
> *RTE continuity announcer after highlights of the Republic's 4-1 home*
> *defeat by Denmark*

That should be the theme song for *Kelly*.
> *2FM's SIMON YOUNG fades out the song 'You Don't Have To Be A Star*
> *To Be In My Show', with a suggestion for the makers of the*
> *BBC chat show*

Heggald o' Heggald!
> *O'Connell Street newspaper vendor during 1985* Evening Press *strike*

Die, maggot-farmer!
> *ARNOLD SCHWARZENEGGER utters the MF word as amended by*
> *Ulster Television's dubbing crew*

And there we must leave Harry Belafonte with his hole in the bucket.
> *RTE continuity announcer fading out 'There's A Hole In The Bucket'*

Who gives a shit about Rita anyway?
> *Radio 1's* An Nuacht *starts with an unscheduled item* as bearla

A top level garda internal inquiry is being held in Connemara into an allegation that a local garda shot a cow . . . There has been no statement from the cow.
> Irish Press *reports on a career at steak, 1985*

Give me a sheep's head, sonny, and cut it as close to the arse as you can.
> *Dublin shopper to butcher, captured on the RTE radio documentary*
> Just Up Your Street

FLOAT THE GOAT'S HEAD
(Clerical Errors)

The word rock and roll comes from the gutter. It means fornicating in a car.

Anti-rock campaigner Fr JOHN O'CONNOR

Young people are urged to go out and get a goat. They are to cut its head off and drain its blood in a cauldron, and float the goat's head.

Fr O'CONNOR passes on a recipe he claims he deciphered from a Rolling Stones record

Much of the contemporary music that is favoured in some quarters is crazy stuff, leading only to gyrations and a lack of personal decorum that borders on the irrational.

Dr JEREMIAH NEWMAN, Bishop of Limerick

Provo in confession box: Father, I bombed a barracks.
Priest: For your penance you must do all the stations.

Fr MICHAEL CLEARY tells a joke. Boom, boom!

Anyone can get a girl to go to bed with him now because far too many girls make sex so readily available now, there's no need for anyone to rape.

Fr MICHAEL CLEARY

THE NEXT U2
(Crystal Ball Gazing)

How much longer can the censor protect film goers from the facts of life with his scissors? . . . How long before the BBC and ITV are showing uncut versions of *The Graduate*?

Irish Times writer KEN GRAY, 1970

I remember them before they went multinational.

ZIG & ZAG at the start of their Earthly career, asked how they'd like to be remembered

The Commitments is my first book and okay, it is limited in its style, but come back when I write three or five.

Future Booker Prize winner RODDY DOYLE

It's already done, it is a *fait accompli*. On June 18th the [Maastricht] Referendum was held and 65% of the people favoured it.

Incoming US Ambassador to Ireland, WILLIAM FITZGERALD, to the US Senate, June 3rd '92, fifteen days before the referendum took place

I've no doubts Cliff Richard is here to stay, so too are Cilla Black, Elvis, The Beatles, Ray Charles and The Bachelors, and I'd like to think The Migel Five will as well.

Commentator JIMMY MAGEE gets it nearly right, 1964

Jump The Gun — they could be the next U2.

Presenter DEREK DAVIS meets his Migel Five

You'd be barred from making love in the Underwater City. We'd be very strict on that to keep the numbers down. If you come to the City you never die. You'd be 2,000 years old and you wouldn't know it. When the world blows up, the Underwater City becomes a flying saucer and leaves the Earth. We'd be able to float around for forty million years. There'd be about three million people in the flying saucer — it'd be a big one. There'd be two of everything — two guards, two priests, two doctors.

Pop singer AIDAN WALSH lays contingency plans for the end of the world

BICYCLES ALL THE TIME
(Occupational Hazards)

You end up being hassled by people talking about bicycles all the time — that's why I stay at home a lot.

Cyclist STEPHEN ROCHE on tyresome fans

There was homosexuality, though I didn't recognise it as such. Nor, I imagine, did most of the guys who were doing it.

Actor GABRIEL BYRNE on his training for the priesthood

The editor of the *Connaught Tribune* called me in. He said he couldn't fire me . . . but he advised me to get out of journalism, or that if I remained in journalism never, ever to tell anybody what happened.

Broadcaster SEAN DUIGNAN recalls being the only journalist admitted to the site of the world's then worst airline disaster, near Galway in the late-Fifties, and not bothering to file a story because it was his day off

If people come up to you at the wrong time, and you're not feeling well, you can get narky with them. People could interpret that as you getting above yourself, but if they are the seventeenth person that day who has shouted a comment about the weather, it does sometimes grate.

RTE Met-man GERALD FLEMING locates an area of high pressure

Shatter! Shatter! Shatter! You're the fella that's going around pushing condoms down everyone's throats.

Alan Shatter TD gets a mouthful while electioneering in Clonskeagh, Dublin

THINGS ALWAYS SEEM TO
GO WRONG
(Sob Stories)

I always do that to people I like . . . Things always seem to go wrong
for me. . . .
> *Footballer VINNIE JONES pleads for sympathy after biting the nose of a*
> *journalist in a Dublin hotel*

Mr Justice Carney said he had drink taken when arrested after gardai
were called to the hotel at 1.45 am. He said he was seeking after-hours
drink after what he described as 'a particularly stressful week's work'.
> Irish Press *reports on a high High Court Judge*

There's nothing lower than someone who robs a robber.
> *MARTIN CAHILL, The General, accuses the IRA of unsporting behaviour*
> *after they try to relieve him of some of his ill-gotten gains*

There's nothing worse than getting squelt on.
> *Criminal interviewed on RTE Radio 1 comes out against 'squealers'*

The Irish nation was so disappointed that I wasn't competing . . . It
was like the President of Ireland dying . . . parliament stopped a session
the day after I pulled out and tried to talk me into running again.
> *Modest EAMON COUGHLAN tells the* Los Angeles Times *how his forced*
> *withdrawal from the 1984 Olympics almost brought the country to its knees*

We were in the wrong place at the wrong time.
> *England football hooligan DAVID O'LOUGHLIN*
> *following his conviction for his part*
> *in a rampage through Dublin*

You're dealing with people who sometimes don't pay you back.
> *OLIVER DONNELLY, Dublin moneylender, charged with extracting*
> *interest rates of up to 248% (his licence was withdrawn)*

LEGS MISSING
(Life's a Pitch)

If in winning the game we only finish with a draw, we would be fine.
JACK CHARLTON

The game in Romania was a game we should have won. We lost it because we thought we were going to win it. But then again, I thought there was no way we were going to get a result there.
JACK CHARLTON after defeat by Bulgaria, 1987

If anybody had called me Turnip Head, I'd 'ave punched his head in.
JACK CHARLTON puts himself in the shoes of besieged England manager Graham Taylor

There was a few legs missing and it showed towards the end of the game.

JACK CHARLTON after 1-3 home defeat by Austria, 1995

March is probably the one month when you cannot predict a result.
JACK CHARLTON, after a disappointing home draw vs Northern Ireland, 1995

I think if we join Europe, the way things are looking we're more likely to have a war with America than anybody else.

Eurosceptic JACK CHARLTON

We fought two wars with the Germans. We probably got on better with the smaller nations like the Dutch, the Belgians, the Norwegians and the Swedes, some of whom are not even in Europe.

JACK CHARLTON

It is true that I don't write letters to people or call them on the phone to tell them they are finished. That, for me, has a ring of finality about it.

JACK CHARLTON

John McGrath. . . .

JACK CHARLTON

Liam O'Brady. . . .

JACK CHARLTON

David Irwin. . . .

JACK CHARLTON

DOGS WITH WORMS
(Eye Of The Beholder)

Nora Bennis is an anagram of 'born insane'.
  In Dublin's *GERRY McCARTHY spells the worst for the Solidarity leader*

The Mullingar Heifer, the Sun City Serenader, Air Lingus's favourite passenger, the one and only Joe Dolan!

Compère at Joe Dolan concert

God would want a remarkably small mind to be calculating what I did with my plumbing.

Gay activist, Senator DAVID NORRIS

Little weasel . . . Mary Kenny without the charlady towel on her head.
MICHAEL D. HIGGINS on Eamon Dunphy

I always thought [Bishop Eamon] Casey was a prick . . . I thought he was a prick since I was about eight and I saw him singing 'Come Back Paddy Reilly' on the *Late Late Show*. I just thought, you know, fuck off!

Novelist RODDY DOYLE

I thought he was going to ride into town on Shergar.
JOHN BOWMAN on writer Gordon Thomas in the aftermath of Thomas's controversial Bishop Casey interview

Mr Paisley has never had a good word to say about anyone other than himself and Jesus Christ, whom he refers to as His Maker — a rather poor testimonial.

Writer JAMES CAMERON

He drives a Capri (very fast) and is in the habit of picking up parking tickets at the rate of one a week. His hobbies include fishing, hurling, horse racing, dog racing and speculation on the stock exchange. Endowed with the gift of the gab, he'd talk a hole through a wall.

Musical Gazette *in praise of Donie Cassidy, 1970*

Archbishop Connell might know a lot about angels but he knows fuck all about fairies.

Senator DAVID NORRIS

Mrs Windsor can come and go as she wants.

GERRY ADAMS on a visit by the Queen of England to Northern Ireland

The little serpent-like Cardinal with the skin of a snake on his face.

Rev IAN PAISLEY on Cardinal Cathal Daly

The Rev Ian Paisley of Bob Martin University. I always thought Bob Martin were pills for dogs with worms.

Senator DAVID NORRIS

John Waters, *fuck* John Waters! I read his book [*Jiving At The Crossroads*] before it came out and I was glad John was doing something useful. I would have thought it would have sold about a thousand copies, so I said it was fine.

Author COLM TOBIN fatigued by questions about his fellow man of letters

Sinead O'Connor is like a stopped clock. She's right twice a day.

Writer LIAM FAY

I'd recognise Big Tom from the bolts in his neck.

Singer COLM C. T. WILKINSON

[Colin Montgomerie] looked like a bulldog licking piss off a nettle.

Golfer DAVID FEHERTY marks the Scotman's card

You're our favourite TV girl and wouldn't you make a lovely lady butcher.

Fan letter to newsreader Anne Doyle

TERMINAL KNITWEAR
(Take Note)

FOR FOX SAKE STOP HUNTING

Sign outside Clonmel garda station

TERMINAL KNITWEAR 1/2 PRICE

Terenure boutique

DRAW TAKES PLACE EVERY SUNDAY MORNING AT 2 PM

Sign outside Castle Inn, Rathfarnham

LIVE DANCING EVERY THURSDAY

Sign, Eyre Square, Galway

MR IAN GOW TD MP

Advertised speaker at Belfast meeting of Friends Of The Union

CULTS: The concierge will direct you to the nearest cult location you belong to.

Room directory in Aer Lingus's Commodore Hotel, Paris

MAIL: Your incoming mail is placed daily in your key hole.

Ditto

SOON

Monitor at Knock Airport announces departure time for flight to Luton

STERLING NOT ACCEPTED. IF SO, 10% CHARGE APPLIES

Texaco station, Dublin

A THOUSAND CAMELS
(Mature Recollections)

I got through to him [President Hillary], I remember talking to him . . . I remember it distinctly.

BRIAN LENIHAN TD

I did not speak to President Hillary. I did not speak to him. That's my mature recollection.

BRIAN LENIHAN TD

We tried very hard that night but the President wouldn't play ball. The bollox. The boy in the park wouldn't function.

NEIL BLANEY MEP recollects the same events

I met him [comedian Mel Smith] first in Barbados and I played it on the piano and he and his wife were in tears.

CHRIS DE BURGH on the universal effects of 'Lady In Red'

RTE and all the newspapers were very corrupt in the early Sixties. There was huge payola. Most of the records played on the radio were played through 'little gifts'.

Impresario NOEL PEARSON

I never took money to bend the truth, or the charts. You had to bend the charts anyway because you'd never have the figures. You tended to favour the people you liked.

SHAY HEALY on working for Spotlight *magazine*

Travelling with The Dubliners, it usually took about three or four hours to get to some part of the country and three or four days to get back.

Broadcaster CIARAN MacMATHUNA recalls the touring schedules of the group whose biggest hit was 'Seven Drunken Nights'

[My mother] was so religious she wouldn't talk to me for six months because I was playing Judas in *Jesus Christ Superstar*. 'Anyone but Judas,' she'd say.

Singer COLM C. T. WILKINSON

Arsenal, Manchester United and Liverpool.
> *Former ace striker BRIAN LENIHAN TD lists the clubs who*
> *unsuccessfully sought his signature*

It was like someone releasing me from prison.
> *Footballer NIALL QUINN on leaving Arsenal*

You had spells when you never knew if you were in the squad. You never got your letter saying you were in the squad until after you got back from an international.
> *Republic defender MARK LAWRENSON on pre-Jack days*

I used to work all through my holidays and that tends to make you very serious from a very early age.
> *MARY HARNEY TD*

One fella offered him a thousand camels for me. We were standing on a pier in Egypt and he besieged me and it went on all day, going up from two hundred camels. And this guy wasn't joking. He already had four wives, so what's a fifth one? So David gets used to this.
> *The trials of being Mr TWINK, as described by the chanteuse*

Mr Hume . . . spoke about Clement Freud who had just lost his Westminster seat. Mr Freud's favourite game was to drink two bottles of Jameson with his brother. Whoever finished his bottle first went outside and knocked and the other had to guess who it was.
> Irish Times

TONS OF FRECKLES
(Ad Hocking)

FOR SALE MALE DONKEY, IN FOAL, CHEAP

Killarney Advertiser

Female seeking professional S or D/W/M, 48-plus, Irish, 6'4", 200 lbs-plus, dark red hair, brown eyes, full beard, moustache, with tons of freckles. Vietnam veteran, enjoys sports cars.

Picky personal ad, Boston Irish News

For immediate sale a 1980 Datsun Saloon 120Y . . . It must have been made from recycled Coca-Cola cans. The body is in terrible condition, the front seating is most uncomfortable . . . Would make ideal chicken coop or suitable for bringing turf from the bog or stunt work in films.

Advert in Kerry's Eye

DRAW IN AID OF GOREY ACTIVITY CENTRE. TICKETS ON SALE HERE: 10 FOR 50p OR 15 FOR £1

Gorey shop sign

One of the most beautiful modern banknotes currently issued, the Irish Punt is a superb piece of engraving. Crisp, uncirculated, only £2.25 or three for £6.25.

'One-for-the-price-of-two' offer on 'Eire punts' in London's
Coincraft *magazine*

The property . . . is adjacent to the new bypass road which passes through the town.

Advert in Irish Times

TRAP-A-FLY. The "ECOLOGICAL" way to catch flies. Flies think they are coming to an "ORGY" when they are really coming to their "FUNERAL" . . . Don't take our word for it that these traps catch flies. Just ask any fly!!

Advert in Evening Press

BISHOP! BISHOP!
(Ulster Says . . .)

The Catholics have been interfering in Ulster affairs since 1641.
Rev IAN PAISLEY

I hope this is not an isolated incident.
Rev IAN PAISLEY reacts to the killing of three IRA members, 1988

There is a risk, and that could be disastrous for everyone in the Isle of Man and Ulster.
Unionist MP JOHN TAYLOR on planned test at Trawsfynydd nuclear plant in Wales

The people of Dublin are equally as British as the English, if not more so.

> *Ulster Protestant candidate Mr MICHAEL BROOKS makes a brave but doomed bid for a Donegal Dáil seat, 1987*

BELFAST SAYS NO . . . EL

> *Season's greetings on official Christmas card from Belfast Lord Mayor, SAMMY WILSON*

If you took the word 'no' out of the English language, most of them would be speechless.

> *The SDLP's JOHN HUME on the Unionist leadership*

Good evening Mr Mallon. What is your name?

> *UDR patrolman stops the SDLP's Seamus Mallon at checkpoint*

Bishop! Bishop!

> *Rev IAN PAISLEY calls his dog*

Saint Patrick was a protestant!

> *Rev IAN PAISLEY*

LIVERS AND LAKES
(Freudian Slips)

It is not acceptable that the Department of Health should pay only lip service to the importance of breastfeeding.

FIONA TIMLIN of La Leche League

I have seen people who have crawled out behind the rocks and behind the stones in solidarity with Brian Lenihan.

Senator SEAN FALLON detects Fianna Fáil support even where the grassroots don't grow

We would like to emphasise that the spirit as well as the letter of our amateur status rules and regulations should be appreciated and honoured by all our units.

GAA report urges members to soldier on

We are organising in the Catholic Church and we hope to get support as well from the opposition churches.

JOE COSTELLO of the Prisoners' Rights Organisation

The future of Dr Fitzgerald's government depends on two DTs.
BBC TV pundit predicts a shaky future for Ireland's coalition

In Ireland we still have one of the best environments in Europe but there have been a number of serious pollution problems in our livers and lakes.
CHARLES HAUGHEY to Ard Fheis

Liars have a stranglehold grip on the Dáil. Three of the opposition parties have liars as their Justice spokespersons and any question of the outmoded aspects of the legal profession being questioned brings liar members into the House in big numbers.
Press statement released by Fine Gael TD GAY MITCHELL

Visitors [to the Maze prison] with parliamentary connections had built up considerable expertise in concealing items in children's nappies, surgical dressings and even the orifices of the body.
The Sun

4.00 NEWS. TOO HIGH A PRICE. Mary Clark investigates the problem of extortion to fund the activities of parliamentary organisations in Northern Ireland.
Irish Times

The party with the most attractive sex reform package . . .
Sunday Tribune *report taxes the imagination*

At the end of the day it is we ourselves, the Authority, the management and the staff who have somehow or other collectively to address the problems and the future and to work out a strategy for the broadcasting service for the 1880s and 1890s.
Incoming RTE Director General VINCENT FINN, in Access *magazine*

Riada & Co Stockbrokers require a Guilt Settlement Clerk.
Gilt-edged opening advertised in Business And Finance

We want to dehumanise the social welfare system.
ALBERT REYNOLDS TD

The name of the attorney who questioned Mrs Bernadette McAliskey
in a Federal court in New York this week during the extradition case
concerning a Crumlin Road escapee, Joseph Doherty, was
Ira H. Bloch.

Irish Times

A whisky museum will open . . . along with restaurants, pub and a
magnificently plastered members' lounge.

Picked up by Irish Times

At the Irish National Bird Show in the Mansion House . . . there will
be a Talking Birds Class. It will be judged by Anne Doyle, the RTE
newsreader.

Irish Times

I GET A CADDY
(Ouch!)

I think that violence within sex is quite common. And attractive and interesting and fun.

Actor PATRICK BERGIN

I'm sick answering questions about the fucking peace process.

Taoiseach JOHN BRUTON, exhausted, fumes

I gather Jim and Meg [Mullion] are heading for the Far East where they plan to spend more time with their money.

The Sunday Indo *with its finger on a paranormal pulse in May 1995. The happily monied couple had been dead for some time*

The next time you are back in Northern Ireland I will have you shot.

ALEX HIGGINS puts NI team-mate Dennis Taylor in the frame after defeat by Canada

The really important thing is that where I race, he doesn't. Otherwise something really serious could happen.

Cyclist ROBERTO VISENTINI dissolves his partnership with team-mate Stephen Roche after Roche beats him to the winning line

If Mullingar's [American-owned] factory closes down, you will be the next to go down. We will get you, be it long or short. You will have a ball of lead wherever you finish up.

Extract from death threat received by Senator Michael D. Higgins, a vocal opponent of Reagan's Presidential visit in 1984

Go back to where you came from.

Fianna Fáil TD NED O'KEEFE across the Dáil chamber to Dublin-born Alan Shatter TD

Stories that might be incriminating to opposition deputies or councillors should be fully checked and forwarded to the Press Officer.

Internal Fianna Fáil document, uncovered and withdrawn 1984

[Garda Walsh] went up to the car and asked Clayton why he had failed to stop . . . Clayton told the garda to quit messing with him — he would do himself a lot of harm. He told Garda Walsh that he didn't have time to be talking to him.

> The Irish Press *reports on a court appearance*
> *at which U2's Adam Clayton was banned from driving*
> *for 2 years for dragging a garda 45 feet*
> *while drunk at the wheel*

Third World food.

> *Minister for Food,* JOE WALSH, *on rice and vegetarian fare*

[Sheffield United manager] Dave Bassett is the cockney cock of the north, just after a nightmare season which left him feeling like an AIDS victim.

> Evening Press *scores an own goal*

Why shouldn't the Pakistan Government look for an Anglo-Pakistan Agreement to look after the Pakis in Bradford?

> *Unionist MP JIM MOLYNEUX*

When I play golf I get a caddy, and Dr Fitzgerald has plenty to do rather than push his wife around in a wheelchair.

> J. J. WALSH, *editor of the* Munster Express, *on the*
> *Taoiseach's schedules, 1986*

DRINK AND PLAY BINGO
(It's A Man's World)

You all have to be a man. Even the ladies have to be a man in that you have to make up your minds.

Justice FRANK ROE advises a jury

One girl was dissuaded from terminating her pregnancy because I got together some gorgeous maternity clothes.

PATSY BUCKLEY of SPUC includes all the options

Find another angle, like a good girl.

Knights of Columbanus spokesman to reporter who asked if the organisation would consider admitting women

What man wants to have anything to do with a girl who has been used and abused by any man who comes along with condoms?

ALICE GLENN TD

Sweet blue eyes will not be a persuasive voting factor.

Dr CYRIL DALY dismisses the prospect of women winning election to the board of the Irish Medical Union

If men would bring into sexual relationships the enthusiasm and finesse they bring to the Gaelic games, it would be great.

Psychologist JUNE QUINN-BERGER

I think the Irish woman was freed from slavery by bingo ... They can go out now, dressed up, with their handbags and have a drink and play bingo. And they deserve it.

Writer JOHN B. KEANE

Some sort of Women's Freedom Day.

International Women's Day viewed through the eyes of
Rev IAN PAISLEY

We must not allow the name of Bridget to be abandoned and must do all we can to bring it back to currency.

Cardinal TOMAS O'FIACH calls for a generation of young Biddies

There is still a high percentage of married women working for no valid reason though they realise that by doing so they are depriving many young people from starting their careers in the civil service, banking or teaching ... These people are not willing to forgo the perks that a second salary can bring, like the trip to the Costa Brava, that second car or that well-stocked cocktail cabinet.

Reverend Brother VIVIEN CASSELS, 1976

There's much that's made of women's rights, in inverted commas, but what about the rights of the children? What about their duties? I mean, you can't wean a calf from a cow overnight.

Fine Gael TD BRENDAN McGAHON

Get married again.

Taoiseach CHARLES HAUGHEY to woman asking for an increase in the widows' pension

I hope you won't ask any silly questions like what's my favourite colour shirt.

DES O'MALLEY TD prefaces an interview with a female journalist from Image *magazine*

BUT YOU TOLD ME TO
(Strange Exchanges)

[A] Russian man and his girlfriend . . . asked in broken English for protection at Shannon Airport duty free shop . . . Security officials were called and they were taken away for interrogation. It was some time before it dawned on the interrogators that the Russians had, in fact, been looking for condoms.

Irish Times

Interviewer: Is it not dangerous to sell people knives called Rambo knives?
Dublin shopkeeper: I wouldn't say so, a lot of them can't spell.

RTE Radio 1

Councillor P. J. Fogarty: I propose that we build a urinal.
Councillor Paddy Burke: I'll second that and propose that beside it we build an arsenal.

Exchange at meeting of Dublin County Council

If you come to the States I'll spit on you.

Noraid supporter writes to Dublin's Lord Mayor, Michael O'Halloran

If you send me the fare I'll gladly let you spit on me.

Mayor posts one-line reply

I was called out to a non-existent phone call. When I returned I lifted my glass, smelled and said 'My god, this is foul. It smells like piss.' A voice from the back called out, 'We know, but whose?'

Wine connoisseur T. P. WHELEHAN recalls a tasteless tasting at Trinity College Dublin

How the hell could they be equal when the woman is made from the rib of man?

Mr FRANK CALLAGHAN of the Amalgamated Engineering Union, asked by John Bowman if men and women are equal

I have no further questions.

JOHN BOWMAN

Jim Duffy [whose taped revelations landed presidential hopeful Brian Lenihan in hot water] recounted a visit to a church where he was immediately set upon by an apoplectic senior citizen who angrily shook a fist and exclaimed, 'You bastard, you fucking bastard!' a number of times. Then, realising that he was in a House of God, the man began groaning 'Oh, fuck, I'm in a church. Oh Jesus, look what you made me do!'

Host Joe Duffy's response to this full and frank version of events was muted, and he hurriedly ushered Jim onto the subject of the threatening letters he had received in the wake of Lenihan's political assassination.

'But you can leave out the bad language,' advised Joe.

'But you told me to leave it in,' protested Jim.

From The Sunday Show, *RTE radio*

Dear Mr Galloway, I thought I was writing to a person of sincerity and reason but I find you are just a typically abusive Trotskyist shit.

Workers' Party TD TOMAS MacGIOLLA to British Labour MP
George Galloway

Please don't write again.

GALLOWAY concludes their correspondence

Myles Dungan: You were very ill as a child, weren't you? Didn't you have TB and mastitis?

Writer Tom McIntyre: I think you mean mastoids.

Irish Times

Is it any wonder there is trouble in the country where Deputy Shatter originated from.

Fianna Fáil TD MATTIE BRENNAN raises the issue of Alan Shatter's
Jewish faith during a Dáil debate

Is it any wonder there is trouble when Deputy Shatter originates that sort of thing.

Deputy BRENNAN's remarks as they appear in the official Dáil record

You fucking bastard.
> *Deputy FRANK AIKEN to Deputy James Dillon during Dáil debate*

You squeaking pig.
> *The same exchange as it appears in the official Dáil report*

SAS RUB OUT IRA RATS
> The Star, *British edition*

SAS SHOOT DEAD THREE IRA MEN
> The Star, *Irish edition*

He [Bishop Casey] has got a penis like any other man.
> *KEVIN O'KELLY on* The Sunday Show

He has *not* got a penis   he's got a hard throbbing rod of maleness.
> *HELEN LUCY BURKE responds on the subject of the bishop's rod*

Compère Derek Davis: You only come up to my chin.
Contestant: Which one?
> *Rose of Tralee, 1995*

Jim Mitchell, TD: You're always mixing me up with someone else.
Ceann Comhairle, Joe Brennan: Yes, I'm always confusing you with that fellow Mitchell.

Judge William Hamill was hearing a bail application from Michael Connors of Belgard Road, Tallaght, who had been sentenced to six months in jail last week. He said he needed to know Connors' exact date of birth . . . When the judge suggested that they check his driving licence, Garda Michael McElgunn said that Connors had swallowed it at Ballyfermot Garda Station last September.
> Evening Press

GUBUs NEEDED! *Loose Talk 2* is being compiled now. We're searching for some top class GUBUs. Please post your contribution today to: Damian Corless c/o Wolfhound Press, 68 Mountjoy Square, Dublin 1. Please provide a source (newspaper clipping, programme title, date etc.) for your material. Include your name, address and telephone number for confirmation.

SOURCES

(ID = In Dublin; IT = Irish Times; HP = Hot Press)

Age Ten Is Generally Accepted In This Business; 01, IT 8/9/84; 02, ID 17/3; 03, HP10/11; 04, IT 17/1/70; 05, ID 18/1; 06, IT 27/5/89; 07, ID 377; 08, ID 20/15; 09, RTE Radio 1, News At One, 26/4/95; 10, Colemanballs; 11, ID 17/11; 12, HP 10/11; 13, IT 31/1/87; 14, ID 17/13; 15, ID 14/1; 16, Colemanballs; 17, HP 13/2; 18, RTE 1, Pat Kenny Show, 28/4/95; 19, ID X-mas Annual, Dec '93; 20, IT 23/6/84; 21, IT 1/3/86; 22, IT 31/1/87; 23, IT 2/2/85; 24, ID 17/7; 25, HP 9/5; 26, HP 13/9; 27, RTE 1 TV Rep. vs N.I. March '95; 28, HP 13/1; 29, HP 14/6; 30, Author; 31, HP 9/17; 32, IT 27/8/88; 33, IT 15/10/88; 34, HP 10/5; 35, Colemanballs 7; 36, HP 12/2 (New Spotlight '71); **Perity With Steeling;** 01, HP 16/10; *02, Homeward Bound,* TV, (HP 13/12); 03, HP 9/4; 04, IT 5/11/93; 05, HP 13/10; 06, HP 13/23; 07, ID 17/14; 08, HP 13/2; 09, UTV, early '80s; 10, IT 6/1/1990; 11, Sunday Times April '95; 12, HP 9/13; 13, Indonesia Times 27/3/95; 14, IT 17/8/91; 15, Colemanballs; 16, IT 16/12/89; 17, RTE Radio 1, *Sunday Show*, 21/5/95; 18, IT 10/1/87; 19, IT 19/2/87; 20, IT 20/8/88; **Risks With Sex;** 01, HP Aug. '86; 02, HP Aug. '86; 03, IT 9/4/88; 04, HP 10/1; 05, ID 379; 06, HP 13/24; **We Are Not Swedes . . .;** 01, HP Nov. '94; 02, ID Jan. '80; *03, Rodney Rice Show,* RTE 1, 13/3/95; 04, ID 18/24; 05, ID 17/10; 06, HP 13/18; 07, IT 28/11/87; 08, HP 10/13; 09, HP 10/11; *10, Dear Me,* M. Nugent; 11, HP 13/23 *(Today Tonight)*; 12, HP 10/16 *(Morning Ireland)*; 13, ID 18/9; **You Have To Be Mental;** 01, Hot Pres 16/22; 02, HP 10/8/89; 03, ID 17/4; 04, IT 16/2/85; 05, Irish Press 27/2/85; 06, Loaded, April '95; 07, *U2: At The End Of The World,* B. Flanagan; 08, IT 27/7/85; 09, ID Xmas Annual '89; 10, Loaded, April '95; 11, HP Nov. '84; 12, HP 13/14; 13, HP 10/20; 14, ID 17/16; 15, IT 8/4/95; 16, HP 10/9; 17, HP 13/16; 18, HP , 11/9; 19, ID Xmas Annual Dec '90; 20, ID 380; 21, HP 18/12/86; 22, HP 8/24; 23, HP 13/18 (Tribune, Sept. '89); 24, HP 12/15; 25, HP 16/10; 26, HP 8/24; 27, ID Xmas Annual Dec. '94; 28, ID 18/22; 29, ID Xmas Annual Dec. '94; 30, ID Xmas Annual Dec. '94; 31, ID Xmas Annual Dec '90; 32, IT 28/5/88; 33, ID Xmas Annual Dec '90; 34, HP 9/1; 35, ID 18/1; 36, ID 18/1; 37, Evening Press 26/4/95; 38, HP 12/2 *(New Spotlight '71)*; 39, HP 14/9; 40, HP 11/3; 41, HP 11/14; 42, HP 12/2 *(New Spotlight '71)*; 43, ID 381; 44, Loaded, April '95; 45, *Boyzone: Our Story* (Boxtree); 46, HP 14/6; **Specialises In Naughty Nun;** 01, HP 16/22; 02, ID 18/4; 03, HP 10/18; 04, HP 11/7; 05, ID 20/6; 06, *Irish Humorous Quotations,* Flanagan; 07, IT 14/11/87; 08, HP 11/17; **What Do You Call A Female Cow?;** 01, IT 14/2/87; 02, HP 10/4; 03, A. M. Corless; 04, Author; 05, HP 8/16; 06, IT 20/7/85; 07, HP 12/22; 08, HP 9/23; 09, Author; 10, HP 9/23; 11, Author; 12, IT 8/3/86; 13, ID Jan. '94; 14, HP 13/13; 15, HP 13/7; 16, HP 10/14; 17, ID 18/14; 18, Liam Mackey; 19, HP 11/24; 20, HP 10/11; 21, HP 11/16; **Speake Swooped Like A Piranha;** 01, ID Xmas Annual Dec. '89; 02, HP 13/8; 03, IT June '95; 04, IrishTimes 23/4/88; 05, ID 18/12; 06, HP 13/10; 07, ID 18/22; 08, HP 9/2; 09, HP 14/10; 10 HP 10/12; 11, IT 6/5/85; **We Call It Bumblefuck;** 01, IT 11/8/84; 02, IT 26/1/85; 03, ID 377; 04, HP 11/6; 05, HP 11/5; 06, HP 14/12; 07, HP 11/7; 08, IT 9/1/88; 09, HP 11/20; 10, IT 13/2/88; 11, ID 18/24; 12, *Eurovision Song Contest,* RTE 1, 1992; 13, ID 18/11; 14, HP 12/2; 15, ID 18/8; 16, IT 21/1/89; 17, ID 17/14; 18, IT 30/1/88; 19, *Facts on*

File: Encylopaedia of the 20th Century; 20, HP 13/14; 21, IT 25/1/85; 22, IT 29/11/86; 23, IT 26/4/86; 24, Irish Press 26/2/85; 25, IT 16/3/85; **Something Wrong In The State Of Holland;** 01, IT 8/6/92; 02, HP 10/8/89; 03, HP 8/16; 04, ID Xmas Annual '94 (Dec. '93); 05, HP 12/15; 06, HP 13/24; 07, ID Xmas Annual '92; 08, HP 12/21; 09, HP 13/10; 10, ID 17/15; 11, IT 21/1/89; 12, ID Xmas Annual '93 ('92); 13, Sunday Independent 9/7/78; 14, IT 5/4/86; 15, *They Are Of Ireland*, D. Lynch; **Everybody Should Try To Get On;** 01, IT Jan. '95; 02, HP 8/20; 03, *Irish Humorous Quotations*, Flanagan; 04, ID 19/6; 05, ID 19/6; 06, ID 17/16; 07, HP 13/1; 08, IT 30/6/84; 09, IT 31/1/70; 10, IT 14/11/92; 11, IT 1/1/70; 12, ID 18/4; **A Detergent Against Crime;** 01, IT 9/2/85; 02, ID 382; 03, *Morning Ireland*, 3/5/95; 04, IT 25/4/87; 05, IT 22/6/85; 06, IT 27/2/88; 07, IT 17/1/88; 08, IT 1/7/89; 09, ID 366; 10, HP 10/20; 11, ID 18/4; 12, HP 9/13; 13, HP 13/18; 14, IT 4/4/95; 15, ID 18/5; 16, IT 24/8/91; 17, IT 25/7/92; 18, IT 9/1/88; 19, IT April '89; **Violence Delays Peace;** 01, ID 360; 02, ID Xmas Annual '92; 03, IT 29/8/88; 04, ID 371; 05, IT 10/11/84; 06, IT 28/1/89; 07, ID 362; 08, ID 377; 09, Dublin Evening News 6/7/89; 10, ID 377; 11, ID 377; 12, ID Mar. '91; 13, HP 12/7; 14, ID 376; 15, IT 9/11/85; 16, IT 9/2/85; 17, IT 18/6/92; 18, ID 360; 19, IT 30/10/84; 20, IT 25/8/84; 21, IT 6/10/84; 22, IT 1/9/84; 23, HP 13/13; 24, IT 1/9/84; 25, IT 25/8/84; **Heggald O' Heggald!;** 01, HP 9/23; 02, ID 18/3; 03, HP 9/11; 04, UTV 1994; 05, HP 11/9; 06, IT 6/10/84; 08, IT 11/6/88; 07, Irish Press 26/4/85; **Float The Goat's Head;** 01, HP 14/2; 02, HP 14/2; 03, IT 14/11/87; 04, HP 13/12; 05, HP 13/8/87; **The Next U2;** 01, IT 5/1/70; 02, ID Xmas Annual (Dec. '90); 03, HP 11/12; 04, IT 8/6/92; 05, HP 13/17; 06, HP 10/18; 07, HP 11/6; **Bicycles All The Time;** 01, HP 13/1; 02, HP 13/1; 03, HP 12/24; 04, ID 20/13; 05, IT 7/2/87; **Things Always Seem Go Wrong;** 01, Evening Press 17/2/95; 02, Irish Press 9/3/93; 03, IT 7/4/84; 04, IT 24/3/84; 05, IT 4/8/84; 06, Evening Press 16/2/95; 07, IT 1/8/87;

Legs Missing; 01, Colemanballs 7; 02 HP 11/20; 03, ID Xmas Annual '92; 04, Network 2, June '95; 05, IT March '95; 06, ID Xmas Annual '92; 07, ID Xmas Annual '92; 08, IT 21/10/90; 09, HP 14/7; 10, HP 13/9; 11, ID Xmas Annual '92; **Dogs With Worms;** 01, ID Xmas Annual (Dec. '94); 02, HP Aug. '86; 03, ID 17/5; 04, HP 12/10 ; 05, HP 17/10; 06, ID 18/9; 07, HP Xmas Special '88; 08, HP 13/14; 09. ID 18/6; 10, IT May '95; 11, ID Xmas Annual '94; 12, HP 9/1; 13, ID 17/13; 14, ID 17/15; 15, HP 12/2 (New Spotlight '71); 16, *Irish Humorous Quotations*, Flanagan; 17, HP 11/7; **Terminal Knitwear;** 01, IT 5/4/87; 02, IT 11/1/86; 03, IT 24/11/84; 04, IT 8/9/84; 05, IT 7/11/87; 06, IT 20/4/87; 07, IT 20/4/87; 08, IT 23/4/88; 09, Author, July '95; **A Thousand Camels;** 01, Daily Star 26/10/91 (ID 362); 02, Daily Star 26/10/91 (ID 362); 03, HP 1990. Re-pub HP 16/10; 04, ID 18/5; 05, HP 14/9; 06, HP 12/22; 07, IT 14/5/88; 08, HP 13/14; 09, *Just For Kicks*, 1991, ed Corless; 10, *George Graham*, King & Willis; 11, HP 10/20; 12, ID 17/7; 13, HP 11/9; 14, IT 20/6/87; **Tons Of Freckles;** 01, IT 20/6/87; 02, IT 19/8/89; 03, IT 12/9/87; 04, IT 4/7/87; 05, IT 16/2/85; 06, IT 8/12/84; 07, Evening Press 9/7/92; **Bishop! Bishop!;** 01, Author, BBC TV; 02, IT 3/9/88; 03, IT 23/1/88; 04, IT 7/2/87; 05, IT 26/12/86; 06, IT 7/3/87; 07, IT 30/9/89; 08, IT 12/1/85; 09, RTE Radio, 17/3/95; **Livers and Lakes;** 01, IT 29/3/95; 02, IT 3/11/90; 03, IT 28/5/88; 04, IT 18/2/84; 05, IT 25/10/86; 06, IT 14/4/90; 07, IT 21/5/88; 08, IT 4/12/84; 09, IT 7/9/85; 10, IT 27/7/85; 11, IT 7/12/85; 12, IT 18/2/84; 13, IT 16/11/92; 14, IT 31/3/84; 15, IT 9/2/85; 16, IT 14/11/87; **I Get A Caddy;** 01, ID 372; 02, IT 17/4/95; 03, Sunday Independent 5/95; 04, IT 26/3/90; 05, IT 20/6/87; 06, IT 18/2/84; 07, IT 1/3/84; 08, IT 14/1/84; 09, Irish Press 12/1/85; 10, IT 27/6/87; 11, Evening Press 30/11/88 (HP 12/18); 12, IT 8/3/86; 13, IT 20/9/86; **Drink And Play Bingo;** 01, IT 12/3/88; 02, IT 14/1/84; 03, IT 6/8/88; 04, IT 10/11/84; 05, HP 10/11; 05, IT 1/3/86; 06, IT 12/10/86; 07, HP 10/13; 08, IT 14/3/87; 09, IT 10/2/90; 10, ID 18/9; 11, HP 11/14; 12, IT 10/6/89; **But You Told Me;** 01, IT 13/10/84; 02, IT14/12/85; 03, M. Corless; 04, IT 5/1/85; 05, HP 13/13; 06, IT 22/12/87; 07, ID 17/10; 08, IT 14/10/89; 09, IT 21/1/84; 10, IT 10/3/84; 11, IT 17/3/84; 12, IT 3/9/88; 13, ID 18/9; 14, RTE Aug. 1995; 15, IT 23/9/89; 16, Evening Press 16/2/95.

Breakfast in Babylon

Emer Martin

They're enmeshed in a bad luck union . . . .

Isolt is a young Irish drifter, catching the magic bus from
Tel Aviv to Paris, floating down to the South of France,
trapped in drugs and dreaming of Dublin.

Christopher is the Hoodoo Man, dealer, king of petty
crime and collector of refugees and winos, on the run from
the police and the Detroit bikers.

*'Heaven is a rainy Sunday morning in Clontarf, a bottle of
Jameson and Breakfast in Babylon to read again. I loved it from
start to finish.'*
Niall Quinn, author of *Welcome to Gomorrah*.

ISBN 0 86327 483 8

Welcome to Gomorrah

Niall Quinn

'Lia gave me a smile from her repertoire of smiles. It had
that touch of fear and bashfulness, like the mountain cat's.
She was all of smiles, of hues of smiles, all the tropical
colours of happiness.
I began to tell her of a mountain cat I had once known,
that spoke to me in English, Irish and Latin. A trilingual
cat. Her face snapped into open bewilderment, and then
she listened. And with disbelieving eyes
she believed all.'

Set mainly in Brazil, with forays into Europe, Niall
Quinn's brilliant new novel is a love story driven by the
pulse of obsession and the primacy of survival.

'[Niall Quinn] is the spiritual successor to Kerouac and
Burroughs.' *Die Rabe*, Germany

'These stories at times ignite with fury at a single spark of
illumination. Demanding and rewarding.' *Library Journal*,
USA

Quinn's skill at evoking atmosphere is often tremendous.
His sense of poverty and of the oppressiveness of work is
of rare depth. Above all, there are few writers who have
captured so well the disintegration of Irishness in the birth
of a new international underclass.' Fintan O'Toole,
Sunday Tribune

ISBN 0 86327 469 9

The Irish Famine
An Illustrated History

Helen Litton

This is an account of one of the most significant — and tragic — events in Irish history. The author, Helen Litton, deals with the emotive subject of the Great Famine clearly and succinctly, documenting the causes and their effects. With quotes from first-hand accounts, and relying on the most up-to-date studies, she describes the mixture of ignorance, confusion, inexperience and vested interests that lay behind the 'good *v* evil' image of popular perception.

Here are the people who tried to influence events — politicians like Peel, public servants like Trevelyan, Quaker relief workers, local committees, clergy and landlords — who wrestled with desperate need, and sometimes gave up in despair. Why did millions of starving people seem to accept their fate without rebelling? Why starvation on the very shores of seas and rivers plentifully stocked with fish?

This is a story of individuals such as Denis McKennedy — dying in Cork in 1846 because his Board of Works wages were two weeks late — and of a society in crisis. It should be read by anyone who seeks a fuller understanding of the Irish past.

Helen Litton took her Master of Arts degree in History at University College Dublin. She is a leading Irish reseracher, editor and indexer.

ISBN 0-86327-427-7

Proverbs & Sayings
of Ireland

Gaffney and Cashman

An illustrated collection of over 1,000 proverbs, sayings and triads (arranged by subject) from all over Ireland.

Apart from their unceasing curiosity as 'words of wisdom', proverbs enable us to peer through the half-door, as it were, and glimpse the attitudes, folk-memories and philosophies of a people. In this collection, little escapes the barb: the priest, the drink, the lover; society, ideas, virtues and vices. But there is also humour and pride, faith and love . . . and the odd word of caution: ' To praise God is proper, but a wise man won't blackguard the devil'!

'We cannot but welcome this clear, bright collection. A book worth having.' (C. O'Danachair, *Irish University Review*)

'A proverbial best-seller!' (*Sunday Press*)

'If you like proverbs, you will love this book.' (*Irish Independent*)

'Over 1,000 fascinating, witty, cynical and totally Irish aphorisms . . . our verbal legacy, reflecting a high sophistication, mature wisdom and a cultivated social sense.' (*Evening Herald*)

'Valuable and entertaining insight into the wisdom and culture of Ireland.' (*The Standard*)

ISBN 0-86327-432-3

Pot Luck
Potato Recipes from Ireland

Nell Donnelly

Pot Luck — Potato Soups, Stews, Chowders, Salads, Oven-baked, Oven-top dishes. . . .

Better known as spuds, praties, or Murphys, the potato has been associated for so long with Ireland it's easy to take it for granted. But boiled or mashed aren't the only alternatives to serving this always-in-season vegetable.

Combining the traditional and the innovative Nell Donnelly exploits the amazing capacity of the potato to lend itself to an incredible range of soups, stews, chowders, salads, oven-baked and oven-top dishes. From a quick and easy Potato and Cheese Pie to the tantalising taste of Frosted Lamb Loaf; from side dishes to main courses, you'll find an imaginative yet simple recipe for every occasion.

In an Introduction Nell Donnelly also delves into the mysterious history of the potato; recounts old-fashioned remedies associated with the potato and shows how, far from being fattening, the potato is packed with vitamins and minerals essential to good health.

ISBN 0-86327-119-7